Seven Drinks (on the Absurdity of Being Human) and Instructions for Their Service

Ty Harvey

ISBN 978-1-64713-888-2

Contents

Introduction

Each of the following drinks is a play on the interaction between bartender and guest. They're meant to question what cocktails can be and give rise to moments that are distinctive and introspective in ways seldom experienced.

There are no detailed recipes for actual drinks here, only scripts for interactions that celebrate the absurdity of being human and guides to creating new contexts, landscapes, and rituals during cocktail preparation and service.

Thanks for spending time with them.

This is a lithograph of an old-time
bartender mixing drinks

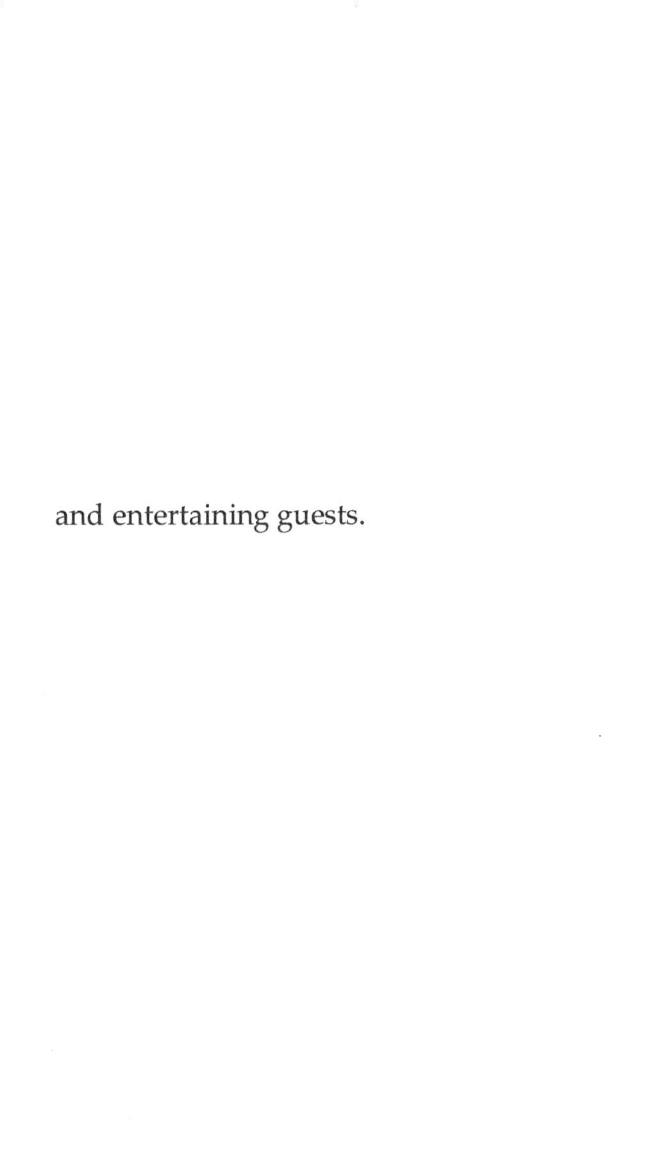

and entertaining guests.

Here the bartender will build a drink behind a screen and then serve the guest a large fishbowl filled with dense fog that conceals the drink inside it. The guest must probe into the fog with a long straw to taste what they cannot see as a forest soundscape emanates from it.

With the guest seated at the bar and ready for their drink, the bartender places a chest-high screen between the guest and the work area. The bartender says to them something like—

"Sounds in the Fog is a cocktail, so it's meant to be enjoyed like any other cocktail. But beyond that, it's an experiment that asks two questions. The first question is: when you taste a drink you can't see, what do you see in your mind when you taste it? The second question is: can a drink be a place, a fleeting, momentary place, instead of a thing?"

The bartender asks the guest if they understand the questions and expounds on any ideas that need clarifying while building the cocktail in the following manner:

Take a large fishbowl and place an empty drinking glass inside it, surrounded by a few smaller glasses filled with hot water. Among it all, save a place for a tiny audio device.

Make the appropriate drink and pour it in the glass in the center. Place the tiny audio device in the fishbowl, playing the soundscape of a night forest.

Take chunks of dry ice and drop them in the hot water of the surrounding vessels. Cover the vessels with mesh or cloth in a way that the fog can escape while there's no chance the guest will consume the dry ice or the water it's in.

Once the fog has enveloped everything so that nothing is visible, the bartender removes the screen between the drink and the guest, slides the fishbowl across the bar, and hands the guest a long straw.

The bartender tells the guest that the drink is in the center of the fog, encourages them to drink it, assures them everything will be fine, and responds to any discussion on the original questions the drink was built to ask.

***

Sounds in the Fog tastes of heavy forest air brightened with long, thin rays of light.

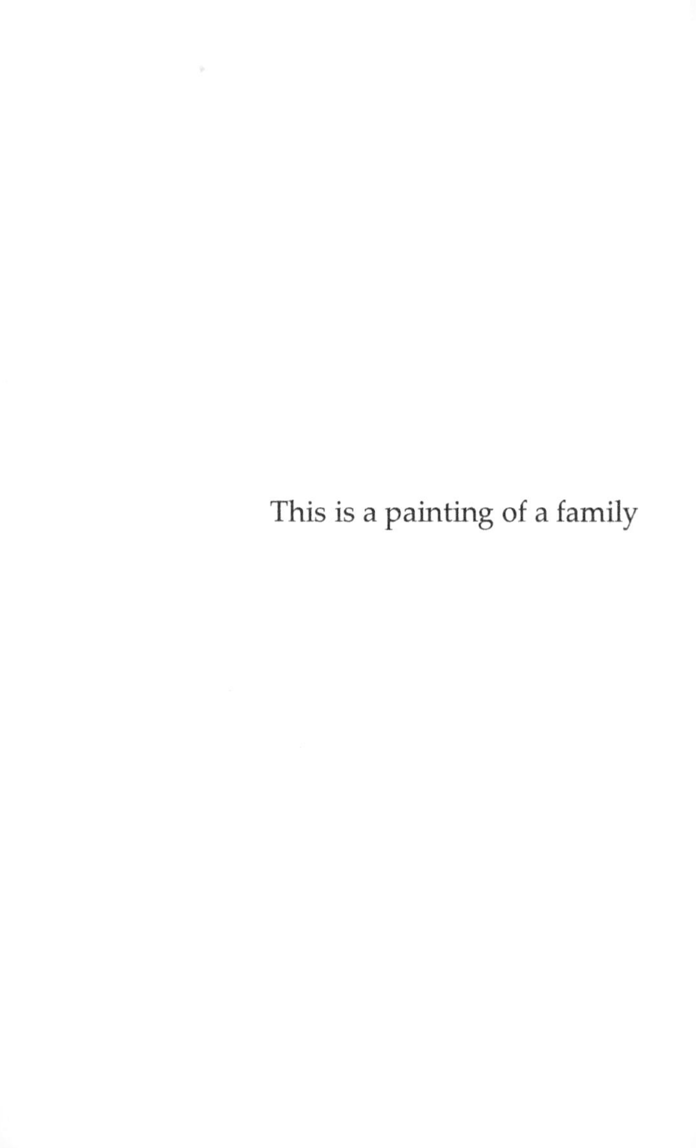

This is a painting of a family

picnicking in a graveyard.

Circle of Salt

Here the bartender will pour a perfect circle of salt using a compass, build a drink inside it, stir it with a stick from a tree in a graveyard, and garnish it with wild sorrel scavenged from nearby.

With the guest seated at the bar and ready for their drink, the bartender clears the bar in front of them and says to them something like—

"Circle of Salt is a cocktail, so it's meant to be enjoyed like any other cocktail. But beyond that, it's an experiment that asks two questions. The first question is: do you believe spirits of the dead exist around us and can affect our lives? The second question is: when faced with a situation where your well-being could be affected if superstition is true, do you reevaluate your beliefs about the spiritual world around you?"

The bartender asks the guest if they understand the questions and expounds on any ideas that need clarifying while building the drink in the following manner:

> Take a string and tie it around a shaker of salt. Hold the string down on the bar with a finger and pull the salt shaker away from it until the string is tight, creating a rudimentary compass. Pour salt on the bar in a perfect circle.
>
> Place a drinking glass in the center of the circle. Take a stick

you picked from a tree at a graveyard and whittle it clean with a knife. Place it to the side. Add a large chunk of ice to the glass. Fill the glass with the appropriate drink ingredients. Stir with the stick from the graveyard while sharing any information known about the lives of those in the graves near the tree the stick came from. Garnish with wild sorrel.

The bartender steps back, leaving the guest to face the drink, and responds to any discussion on the original questions the drink is built to ask.

Circle of Salt tastes of old medicine mixed with a much needed vacation, like a sunny afternoon at a gravesite.

This is a 17th-century print of a doctor
wearing a beak-shaped mask filled
with potpourri to

protect him from the plague.

Bubblegum Balloon

Here the bartender will build a bubblegum-flavored drink in a stemmed glass, covered with a balloon inflated with pungent air. Served with a pincushion, the balloon releases a foul odor when popped before the guest tastes the drink.

With the guest seated at the bar and ready for their drink, the bartender says to them something like—

"Bubblegum Balloon is a cocktail, so it's meant to be enjoyed like any other cocktail. But beyond that, it's an experiment that asks two questions. The first question is: when you have to destroy one thing to gain access to another, does the loss of the first thing affect your perception of the other? The second question is: does the introduction of a fleeting odor affect your perception of a flavor that follows?"

The bartender asks the guest if they understand the questions and expounds on any ideas that need clarifying while building the drink in the following manner:

> Take an empty hand pump sprayer and fill it with crumbs of extremely pungent cheese. Take a large-mouth balloon and inflate it with foul air using the sprayer, tying it temporarily closed with a bread tie.

> Make the appropriate drink and pour it in the glass. Take the balloon filled with foul air and

place the mouth of the balloon over the glass while losing as little air as possible.

The bartender places the drink in front of the guest, along with a pin cushion and pins, and responds to any discussion on the original questions the drink is built to ask.

***

Bubblegum Balloon tastes of childhood nostalgia piercing the unpleasant realities of time's passing.

This is a painting of a cottage in the
snow, created in a community art class

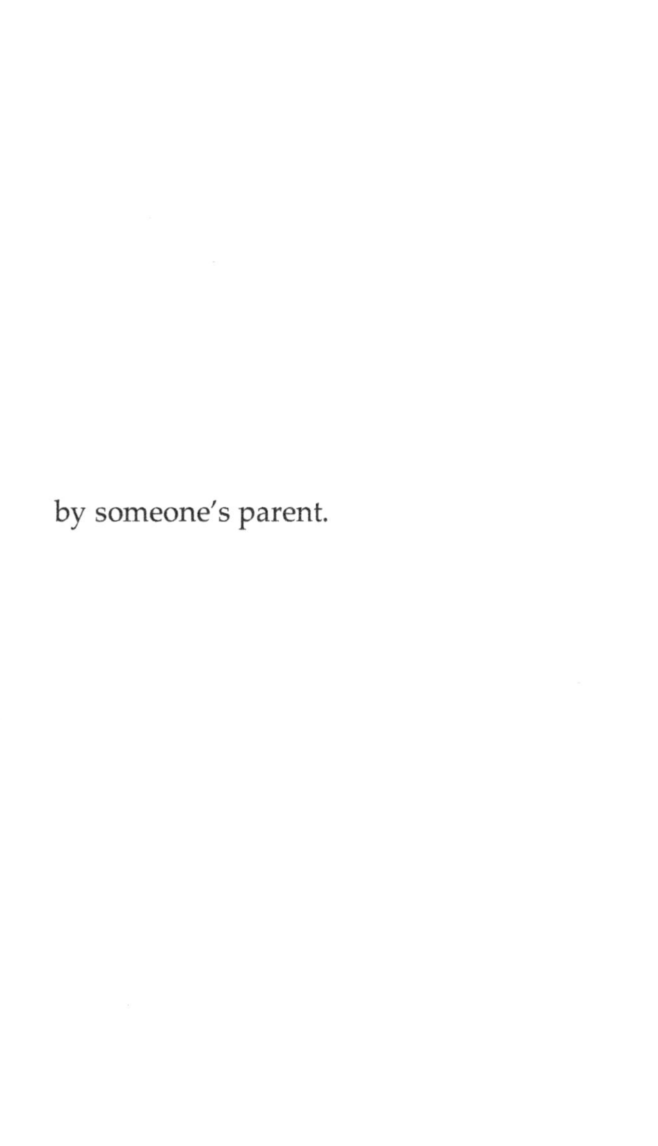

by someone's parent.

Snow Day

Here the bartender will build a drink reminiscent of a snow globe. They will serve it to the guest with a huge wreath and a musical holiday card, preferably out of season.

With the guest seated at the bar and ready for their drink, the bartender says to them something like—

"Snow Day is a cocktail, so it's meant to be enjoyed like any other cocktail. But beyond that, it's an experiment that asks two questions. The first question is: do celebrations stem from human instinct or are they part of our civilization? The second question is: when celebrating a specific season, do flavors not associated with that season taste somehow different than they normally would?"

The bartender asks the guest if they understand the questions and expounds on any ideas that need clarifying while building the drink in the following manner:

> Take a small ceramic cottage and put it in a glass. Pour the appropriate drink over it. Sprinkle silver edible glitter in the drink. Stir.

The bartender places a wreath on the bar, puts the drink in the center, and stirs it one last time to make the glitter swirl. They hand the guest a holiday card that plays music when opened.

***

Snow Day tastes of anything but Christmas.

This is a faded photograph of a Civil
War–era military drummer, with
hands and sticks

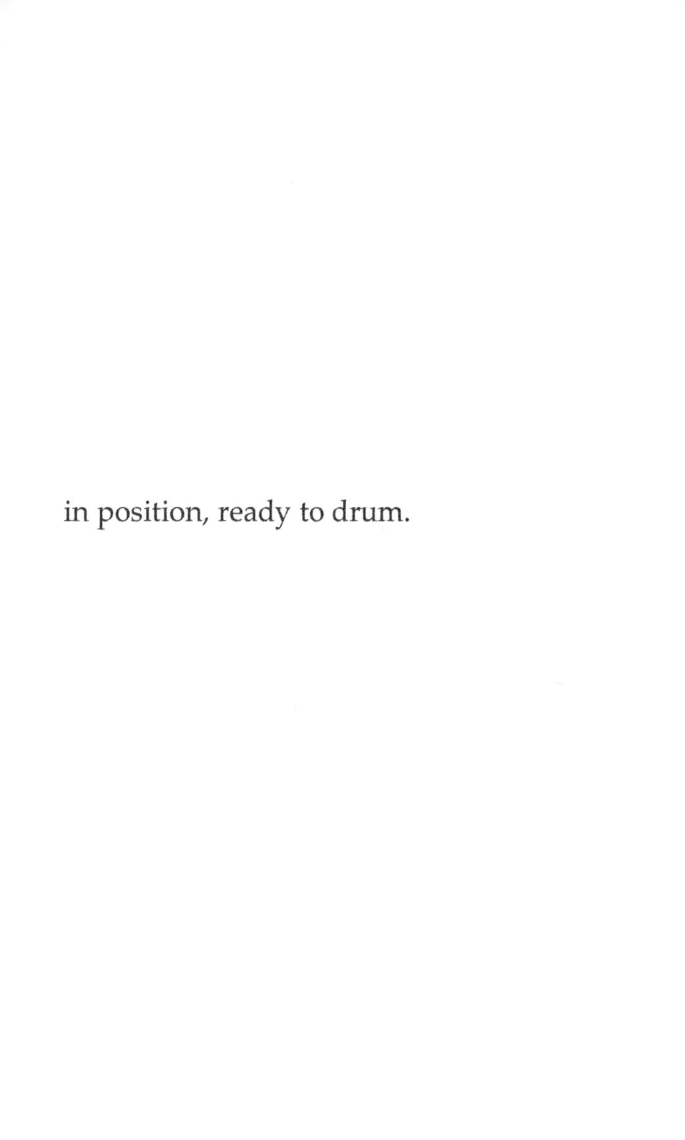

in position, ready to drum.

Tequila Drumroll

Here the bartender will build an extremely spicy tequila cocktail and play a drumroll leading up to the instant the guest takes their first drink.

With the guest seated at the bar and ready for their drink, the bartender brings out a drum and cymbal and says to them something like—

"Tequila Drumroll is a cocktail, so it's meant to be enjoyed like any other cocktail. But beyond that, it's an experiment that asks two questions. The first question is: does setting time aside for a ritual connect you to an inherently human experience shared by everyone? The second question is: does a flavor on your tongue resemble a sound in your head when there's suddenly nothing to hear?"

The bartender asks the guest if they understand the questions and expounds on any ideas that need clarifying while building the drink in the following manner:

> Pour the appropriate drink in a glass. Pour a pinch of salt in a second glass. Prepare the drum, cymbal, and sticks.

The bartender places the drink and salt in front of the guest and directs them to pour the pinch of salt on their tongue. While the salt dissolves in their mouth, the bartender explains that they are going to begin a drumroll and that the guest is welcome to taste the drink as soon as they are ready.

With the guest's mouth dry from salt, the bartender begins the drumroll. When the guest tastes their drink, the bartender hits the cymbal with a loud crash.

The bartender responds to any discussion on the original questions the drink is built to ask and serves the guest ice water.

***

Tequila Drumroll tastes of the sting of knowing the end is coming, mixed with the sweetness of getting a second last breath.

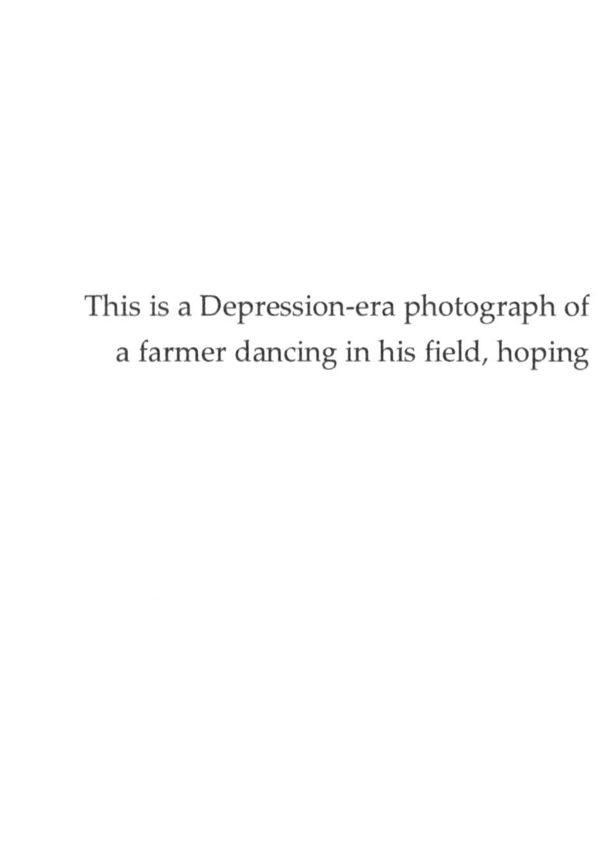

This is a Depression-era photograph of
a farmer dancing in his field, hoping

to bring rain.

Skeptical Winner

Here the bartender will shuffle a glass of spirit among glasses of vinegar and will mix the guest's choice into a drink, for them to taste to see whether they chose correctly.

With the guest seated at the bar and ready for their drink, the bartender places three empty vessels in front of them. The bartender says to them something like—

"Skeptical Winner is a cocktail, so it's meant to be enjoyed like any other cocktail. But beyond that, it's an experiment that asks two questions. The first question is: when you taste a drink for a certain unwanted ingredient (or listen intently to your surroundings for a certain annoying sound, or look far into the distance for a certain offensive thing), to what degree does searching for that unpleasantness change your awareness of what is really there? The second question is: does the weight of a stone in your hand change your perception of the weight of other things, such as the drink in your mouth?"

The bartender asks the guest if they understand the questions and expounds on any ideas that need clarifying while building the cocktail in the following manner:

> Fill one small glass with spirit and the other two with very pungent vinegar. Have the guest smell the vinegar in its

bottle. Cover the glasses with metal tins. Ask the guest to do their best to follow the tin covering the spirit because the drink will be built from what they choose, and if they choose the vinegar, it will ruin everything.

Once the guest makes their choice, mix the appropriate drink.

The bartender pours the drink in a glass containing a large cold stone and tells the guest that they hope they chose correctly.

***

Skeptical Winner tastes of a dry field of ripening fruit, with the bittersweet sight of a beautiful dusk with still no chance of rain.

This is a portrait of an unknown
woman wearing a hat adorned with
very long feathers and sitting in a
chair while

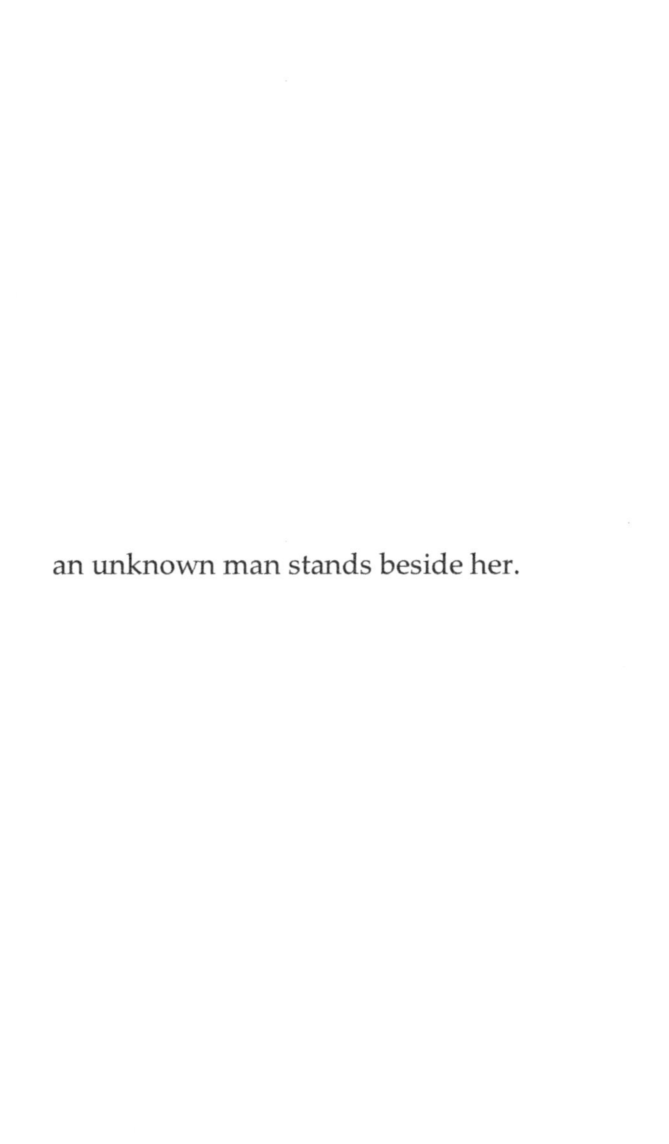

an unknown man stands beside her.

A Chair in a Room with No Chairs

Here the bartender will remove a new folding chair from a box for the guest to sit in while they drink a beer.

With the guest seated at the bar and ready for their drink, the bartender takes out a box containing a brand-new chair. The bartender says to them something like—

"A Chair in a Room with No Chairs is a beer, so it's meant to be enjoyed like any other beer. But beyond that, it's an experiment that asks two questions. The first question is: since the first places to sit in humanity were not chairs but logs and rocks and bare ground that naturally occurred, is a chair a place, a portable place, more so than a thing? The second question is: when you're the only person sitting while others must stand, do you share a momentary kinship with the first person to ever sit in a chair?"

The bartender asks the guest if they understand the questions and expounds on any ideas that need clarifying while building the drink in the following manner:

> Place a bottle of beer in a salted ice bath until the drink is barely above freezing. Take the box containing the chair, cut it open, and take the chair out. Assemble it if necessary. Ask your guest where they would like the chair to be placed in the room. Place it where they

choose, in a room with no other chairs, and invite them to sit.

The bartender goes back to the bar, gets the nearly freezing bottle of beer, pours it into a chilled glass, places a probe thermometer in the drink to demonstrate to the guest just how cold the beer is, returns to the sitting guest, and hands it to them. The bartender tells them to enjoy the chair and their beer.

***

A Chair in a Room with No Chairs tastes of unassuming simplicity, half-dressed or naked, like sitting on the

side of a bed, staring at your own
shadow.

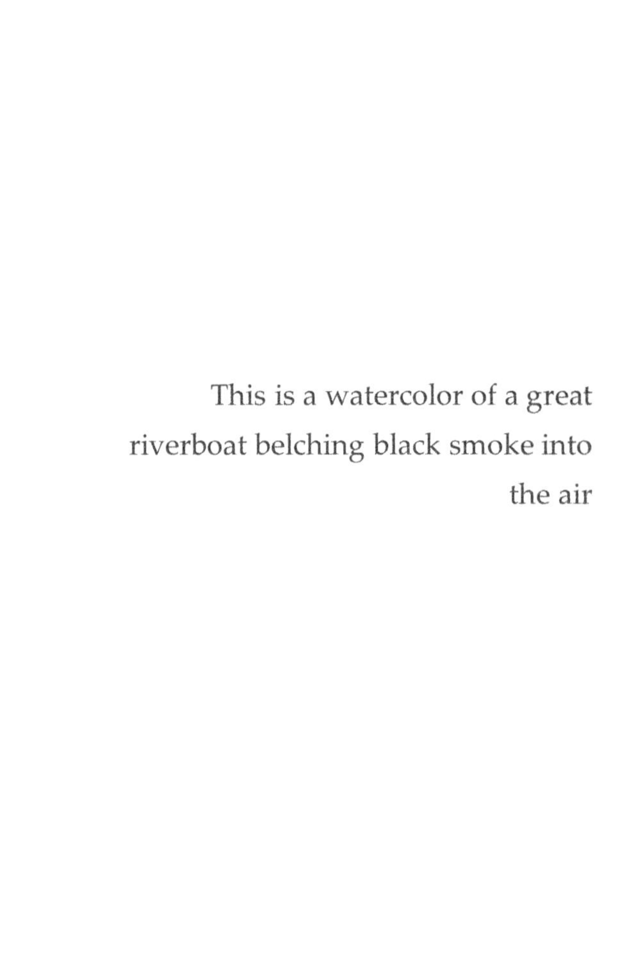

This is a watercolor of a great
riverboat belching black smoke into
the air

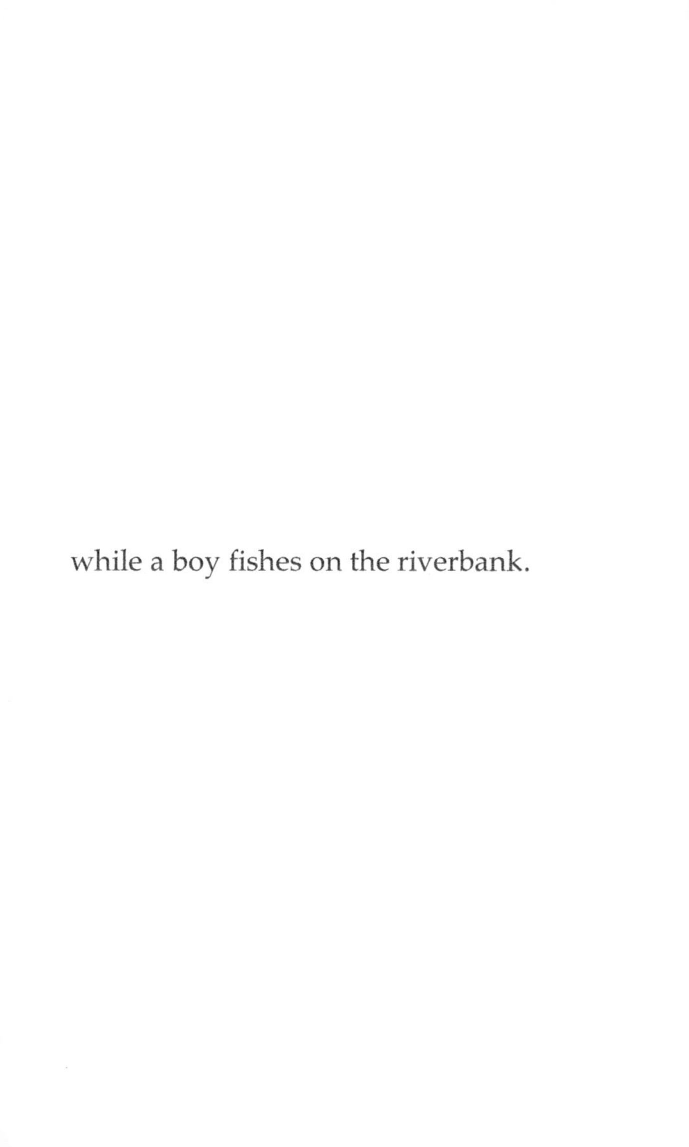

while a boy fishes on the riverbank.

Ty Harvey is a longtime bartender at the Volstead Lounge in Austin, the notorious Eastside home of raucous dance parties and the renowned experimental music showcase Me Mer Mo Monday. He finds life most fascinating when faced with absurd concepts, experiments of perception, and new ways to see the world around us.

9 781647 138882